America's Westward Expansion

Cattle Ranching
in the
American West

Christy Steele

WORLD ALMANAC® LIBRARY

Please visit our web site at: www.worldalmaclibrary.com
For a free color catalog describing World Almanac® Library's list of high-quality books
and multimedia programs, call 1-800-848-2928 (USA) or 1-800-387-3178 (Canada).
World Almanac® Library's fax: (414) 332-3567.

Library of Congress Cataloging-in-Publication Data

Steele, Christy, 1970-
    Cattle ranching in the American West / by Christy Steele.
        p. cm. — (America's westward expansion)
    Includes bibliographical references and index.
    ISBN 0-8368-5787-9 (lib. bdg.)
    ISBN 0-8368-5794-1 (softcover)
    1. Cattle—West (U.S.)—History. 2. Ranching—West (U.S.)—History.
    3. Ranchers—West (U.S.)—History. I. Title.
    SF196.W47S74   2005
    636.2'13'0978—dc22   2004056769

First published in 2005 by
World Almanac® Library
330 West Olive Street, Suite 100
Milwaukee, WI 53212 USA

Copyright © 2005 by World Almanac® Library.

Produced by: EMC—The Education Matters Company
Editors: Christy Steele, Rachael Taaffe
Designer and page production: Jennifer Pfeiffer
Maps and diagrams: Jennifer Pfeiffer
World Almanac® Library editorial direction: Mark J. Sachner
World Almanac® Library art direction: Tammy West
World Almanac® Library production: Jessica Morris
World Almanac® Library editors: Monica Rausch, Carol Ryback

Photo credits: Colorado Historical Society: 26, 28, 32, 34; Courtesy Central Pacific Railroad Photographic
History Museum © 2004, CPRR.org: 35; Denver Public Library Western History Collection: 37, 43; Library
of Congress: cover, 4, 6, 7, 9, 10, 12, 16, 17, 21, 23, 24, 25, 31, 33, 39, 40, 42; National Archives: 36; North
Wind Picture Archives: 13, 18, 19, 22.

Printed in Canada

1 2 3 4 5 6 7 8 9 09 08 07 06 05

Contents

First Cattle in North America

Native Americans lived on the land for thousands of years before Anglos, or people of non-Spanish, European descent, arrived in the American West. Some Native groups had permanent settlements, while others moved with the seasons to hunt, fish, and farm—relying on massive herds of free-grazing buffalo for much of their daily needs. The pattern of Indian life changed forever when the growing Anglo population of the United States began its process of westward expansion.

The era of U.S. western expansion is generally regarded to have begun in 1803, with the Louisiana Purchase, and ended in 1912, when Arizona

◀ Native Americans, such as this Sia buffalo dancer in 1926, prayed for successful buffalo hunts. Buffalo dances were sacred traditions because the Indians relied so heavily on buffalo for their livelihood.

and New Mexico became states. During this period, as more Anglo settlers established settlements on Native American lands, U.S. troops forcibly moved the Indians to reservations. Native Americans also saw their hunting grounds depleted by the growing Anglo population, and buffalo were hunted almost to extinction.

Manifest Destiny—the belief that Americans' God-given right was to take over the continent, spreading U.S. ideas and government to new peoples and territories along the way—shaped U.S. land policy during this era. To achieve Manifest Destiny, the United States purchased land from other countries or conquered territory by taking land from Native peoples until its borders stretched from coast to coast.

The removal of buffalo and Native Americans from their homelands opened huge expanses of grazing land in Texas and the Southwest, and Anglo ranchers seized the opportunity to fill the land with cattle. The huge U.S. cattle boom lasted from the end of the Civil War (1861–1865) until the late-1880s. The expansion of railroad lines during this time made it possible for the first time to ship meat from grazing grounds in the Southwest to markets on the East and West Coasts.

First Cattle in the Western Hemisphere

In 1492, Christopher Columbus became the first documented European to reach the Americas. He landed in what is now the Bahamas and claimed the land for Spain. The islands became the first part of "New Spain," an area the Spanish would come to control that would stretch from present-day Peru to California.

When Columbus returned to Spain, he reported that no horses or cows existed in the Americas. In Spain, cattle ranching and horse breeding were an important part of life. Cattle provided

▶ An artist's 1893 re-creation of Columbus and his crew claiming their landing site for Spain. Columbus soon realized that no cattle or horses roamed the island.

food as well as valuable hides and tallow, or animal fat. Due to their importance, the Spaniards sent livestock to New Spain.

On Columbus's second trip to the Americas in 1493, he landed in present-day Dominican Republic with thirty-four horses and an unknown number of cattle—the first of these creatures in the Western Hemisphere. The Spanish spread the practice of raising cattle and horses to each new settlement they founded, beginning in the islands today known as the West Indies. The livestock thrived, and soon there were more animals than needed for local consumption. Spaniards let these livestock run wild. Native peoples captured the wild cattle and sold smoked meat to sailors on passing ships.

Spanish Cattle Reach Mexico

The Spanish successfully invaded North America in 1519, when Hernando Cortés landed with soldiers and sixteen horses in what is now Vera Cruz, Mexico. Native Americans had never seen horses and feared the animals they called "big dogs." The horses gave Cortés and his men a wartime advantage during his brutal conquest of the Maya and Aztecs, two Native peoples of Mexico. Cortés conquered these civilizations, took their gold, land, and jewels, and forced American Indians to work as slave labor for the Spaniards. To help keep their military supremacy, the Spanish outlawed Native Americans or slaves from owning horses.

Spanish settlers began arriving while Cortés was conquering present-day Mexico. The first cattle landed near what is now Tampico in 1521 with the arrival of Gregorio de Villalobos, the lieutenant governor of New Spain. Conditions in Mexico were even better for cattle raising than those in the West Indies, and one Spaniard named Muñoz Camargo described the population explosion, saying that cattle were "multiplying unbelievably; you cannot exaggerate their numbers or imagine the spectacle before your eyes."

▲ Native Americans—most converted to Catholicism by Spanish missionaries—served as the first cowboys. Centuries later, descendants of these original cowhands, such as this 1905 Jicarilla cowboy, also worked with cattle.

Spanish Ranches in New Spain

Ranching was essential to the expanding Spanish frontier. Spanish settlers raised livestock for food in isolated areas and traded tallow and hides for European manufactured goods.

The Spanish had two main kinds of ranches in New Spain. The first was the mission, a church complex that served as a Spanish frontier institution throughout what is now Mexico, Texas, California, New Mexico, and Arizona. Mission priests tried to convert Native Americans to Catholicism and supported themselves by using converts as slave labor for ranching and farming. Every mission had herds of livestock. Taking care of cattle was viewed as beneath the Spaniards' dignity, and the

Spanish Cattle Breeds in New Spain

Many scholars believe that three Spanish cattle breeds were shipped together to New Spain beginning in 1519. One kind was the black Andalusian fighting bull. This male cow was used mainly for the sport of bullfighting.

The second breed was the white-and-black piebald cow, and the third was the tan-and-reddish Jersey cow with its long, thin head. Throughout the years, the Spanish allowed these two kinds to interbreed with each other, and their descendants—the Texas longhorns —were later made famous during the U.S. cattle boom.

The Texas longhorn had long, pointed horns, big ears, a long head, long legs and tail, narrow sides, and a swayed back. It was a strong animal that outwalked most other cattle breeds and could survive for several days without drinking water. Wild longhorns could also be dangerous and used their long horns to attack people who came near. The horns also made it hard to ship the cattle by railroad car when that method of moving cattle became popular in the 1880s, so the horns were often trimmed first.

priests most often trained non-Spaniards, such as African slaves or their American Indian converts, to do the hard work.

The second kind of ranch was an encomienda, which Spain created with a land-grant system. Spain still owned title to the encomienda land it granted but gave control of its use to a Spanish leader called an encomiendo. The encomiendos had to obey Spain's laws and pay taxes to the Spanish crown.

Encomiendos used Native peoples as slave labor for their ranches. When Cortés first conquered Mexico, he divided the Indians of central Mexico among Spanish leaders. In return for their long hours of hard labor, Spanish law required that encomiendos give food, shelter, clothing, and Catholic religious instruction to Native workers. Spaniards also imported African slaves to work in New Spain.

The Mesta

The Spanish practiced open-range ranching. In this system,

cattle wandered unrestrained to find their own food and water. Under Spanish law, grazing rights were nonexclusive, which means that cattle could freely graze on common ranges, and ranchers were not allowed to keep another rancher's cattle off their land grant. The open-range method of ranching created problems, however, since herds often trampled the crops of farmers. Farmers complained to Spanish leaders and asked that laws be created so that encomiendos had to keep cattle restrained during the growing season. Disputes also arose about cattle ownership. Many encomiendos created brands—special marks burned on the hides of cattle —to show their ownership of the animals, but arguments arose about who owned unbranded cattle. Sometimes, a Spaniard would claim that all unbranded cattle belonged to him.

In 1529, to keep peace and settle these disputes, the Spanish created the Mesta, a stockowner's association that established laws to protect ranchers and farmers. Any person who owned more than three hundred livestock had to join the Mesta and attend its two yearly meetings in February and August. Mesta members had to pay fines for disobeying any rules. The Mesta required that each rancher create a unique brand that would be registered in a master book kept in Mexico City, New Spain's capital.

The Mesta decreed that ranchers round up their cattle twice each year before the Mesta meetings and separate other owners' cattle from their herd. Cattle with different brandings would be returned to their proper owners at the Mesta meetings. To move or sell cattle, the stockowner had to receive a permit from the Mesta.

▲ The branding iron used by Montana's Quarter Circle "U" Ranch in the 1930s. The first recorded branding of animals and slaves (using paint or pine tar) probably occurred in the Middle East more than four thousand years ago. The Spanish brought the practice of cattle branding to the Americas. The tradition of hot-iron branding continues on many present-day ranches.

Chapter 2

Early Ranching in North America

I n the 1600s, people from other European countries began settling in North America. The French started colonies in Canada and along the Mississippi River, including New Orleans. The English founded thirteen colonies on the East Coast of North America, which later became the United States. Like the Spanish, these European colonists also brought livestock with them. Soon, breeds of French cattle and English cattle dotted the North American landscape.

Most of the new European settlers in the North, however, did not practice the same type of livestock raising as the

◀ Early Anglo-European settlers housed their cattle in corrals, or fenced-in enclosures, like this one shown in the 1880s.

North America in 1783

BRITISH TERRITORY

(Ceded to Spain by France, 1763)

Spanish Possessions

NEW SPAIN

UNITED STATES

Pacific Ocean

Atlantic Ocean

Gulf of Mexico

LEGEND
- British Territory
- Spanish Possessions
- United States
- River
- Present-day State Borders

◀ This map shows the territories in North America in 1783. Borders of present-day U.S. states are shown for purposes of reference.

Spanish, and in the 1600s, the word *ranch* was not yet even in their vocabulary. The settlers mainly farmed and supplemented their food supply by raising livestock, such as cattle, goats, sheep, chickens, and pigs. Northern farmers herded cattle by foot. They kept livestock in fenced pastures or let cattle roam nearby fields during the day and herded them into corrals or barns at night.

Cattle was an important industry in the South from the late 1700s. Along with farming crops, such as cotton, Southern plantations raised livestock herds on a larger scale than in the North and herded cattle on horseback. Plantation owners often trained slaves, known as cow hunters, to herd and search for stray cattle. Some of the first African American cowboys probably descended from these Southern cow hunters.

The Hacienda System

Even though other European settlers also brought cattle to North America, it was the Spanish who established the North American ranching industry. Beginning in the 1600s, Spain began the *hacienda* system of land use. The Spanish king offered to sell full

▲ Artist William Henry Jackson's 1880s rendering of a scene from a typical ranching hacienda in Mexico. Haciendas were like small towns in themselves—they included the ranchero's home, vaquero homes, stables, a mill, and sometimes a church and a blacksmith.

titles to land in New Spain, including present-day Mexico, Texas, California, Arizona, and New Mexico. This system created the first private ranches in North America.

Wealthy Spaniards bought land for creating huge business estates called haciendas, which were used for mining, lumbering, farming, or ranching. Less wealthy Spaniards bought modest amounts of land and founded smaller ranches called *ranchos*. The modern word "ranch" originated from the Spanish word *rancho*. The Spanish owners of large ranchos or haciendas were called *rancheros, patróns,* or *dons,* and they ruled their territory like kings.

Until the 1800s, ranchers in present-day Texas, New Mexico, and Arizona had plenty of cattle but no large market in which to sell them. They could not butcher cattle and ship the meat to far-away markets without it spoiling because railroads had not yet been invented. Since meat was not yet valuable, ranchers at this time raised cattle mostly for hides and tallow. To make money on hides and tallow, ranch owners needed huge herds, large amounts of free grazing land—15 to 25 acres (6 to 10 hectares) were needed to support one cow—and a work force of trained *vaqueros*, or "cowhands", who were often Native American.

By the 1600s, however, there were no longer as many Native Americans in New Spain to use as slave labor. Thousands had died from diseases the Spaniards brought with them from Europe, such as smallpox and measles. The ranch owners then had to find and pay for a new vaquero labor force.

The Vaquero

By the 1600s, vaqueros were paid but were more like indentured servants than slaves. Some were former mission Indian converts, but most were Mexicans or *mestizos*, people of Spanish and Native American descent. Others were free African Americans or *mulattos*, people of African and European descent. The American cowboys' job descended from these cowhands' traditions.

Most vaqueros spent their lives on just one hacienda or rancho. They had accounts with the ranch owner and used credit to pay rent for shelter and buy supplies, such as clothing and food. The few wages that a vaquero earned, usually about $15 to $20 each month, were applied toward his debts, and often a vaquero never received any actual money during his lifetime. The vaquero's debt was passed to his children when he died, and so they had to work for the ranch owner, too.

Some vaqueros formed bands and hired themselves to ranch owners during roundups or if ranchers needed to move some cattle long distances from the northern frontier to sell in more populated areas in southern Mexico. Some bands of vaqueros, however, were outlaws tired

▼ Western artist Frederic Remington illustrated the traditional dress of a Mexican vaquero. The word *vaquero* comes straight from the vaquero's best friend—*cattle*. The word *vaca* means cow in Spanish, and vaquero developed from *vaca*.

of performing hard work for almost no wages. They raided haciendas and stole cattle. Most ranch owners only hired these vaqueros if they were desperate for trained help.

Skilled vaqueros were excellent riders with thorough knowledge of cattle behavior. Vaqueros braided horsehair to make ropes and used their amazing roping skills to catch cattle for branding and slaughtering. They used lances or poles to separate cattle from the herd. With long hocking knives, they cut the cattle's tendons, which brought the animals crashing helplessly to the ground to be killed. Vaqueros rode for long hours on horseback, herding cattle during long cattle drives.

Even with their advanced skills, many of the Spanish viewed vaqueros as poor laborers on horseback, and they had few rights. For example, the Mesta ruled in 1574 that no Native American, mulatto, or mestizo vaquero could own a horse, so ranch owners supplied mounts for them. Some vaqueros wanted to be paid in cattle so that they could someday own their own small ranches, but the Mesta stopped these dreams by outlawing livestock payments. If the Mesta rules were broken, the vaqueros would be whipped or have their ears sliced from their head for the second offense. Most vaqueros owned just their saddles and their clothes.

Ranch Life in the Hacienda System

Some Spanish ranch owners lived in large houses in towns and hired Spanish supervisors to oversee ranch operations. Other rancheros built whole communities that resembled small towns on their haciendas. Buildings were constructed around a central courtyard. The largest building was the luxury home of the owner. Smaller buildings might include stables for their horses, a mill for grinding grain, or huts or bunkhouses to house their workers. Some large haciendas also had churches, blacksmiths, and quarters for other craftspeople, such as clothmakers.

Ranchers continued the biannual roundups established by the Mesta in the 1500s. Vaqueros from several ranches worked together to gather thousands of cattle. They often rode in moonlight when the cattle were most active and drove the cattle toward a fixed location from all directions. Once the herd was in one place, vaqueros branded new calves and separated other ranchers' animals from the herd.

During the spring roundup, vaqueros slaughtered cattle for hides and tallow. This process was called *matanza.* Vaqueros herded groups of up to one hundred animals at one time to *calaveras,* isolated places near brooks or forests. Vaqueros roped and killed the animals and then harvested their hides, tallow, and meat.

Branding and Earmarking

Ranch owners from the days of Spanish ranching to today have used brands burned into an animal's hide, usually the left flank, to identify the cattle they own. Each ranch has its own unique brand, which ranges from pictographs, to initials of the owners, to a combination of symbols and letters and numbers. Brands read from top to bottom and from left to right.

At first, Texas settlers used their initials as brands. Later, cattlemen and ranch corporations designed creative brands and forged the design into iron-stamp brands.

Some ranch owners also earmark their animals to further aid identification. Earmarks are designs, such as triangles, cut into the ears of animals.

The cattle bones and entrails were left in calaveras, and wild animals feasted on the remains. The matanza made food so plentiful that the grizzly bear population increased. Grizzly hunting soon became popular among vaqueros, especially in California, and they captured the huge bears with their ropes. On special occasions, the Spanish staged fights to the death between grizzlies and bulls in bullrings.

Chapter 3

Ranching under New Spain and Mexico

As Spanish-controlled territory grew and New Spain's borders spread northward, the Spanish ranching system spread as well, eventually reaching what is now the U.S. Southwest. Cattle ranching reached present-day New Mexico in 1598, Texas in 1690, and then California in 1769.

Most of Spain's large ranching operations were in the sparsely populated northern frontier regions of northern Mexico, Texas, and California. These areas lacked the water supply needed for farming, but the mild climate and acres of wild grass and plants made

◄ This Pueblo Indian man, pictured here in the 1890s, is using a Spanish-style lasso. The Pueblo Indians of New Mexico first learned roping skills in Spanish mission ranches.

them ideal for cattle raising. Despite the region's prime conditions for cattle, New Spain lacked the financial resources and population to develop its northern frontier, so at first, priests in church-funded missions conducted most ranching efforts.

Ranching in Las Provincias Internas

Beginning in the 1700s, the Spanish established missions in what is now the U.S. Southwest. Priests began teaching their converts how to be vaqueros. Not all Native Americans in the region, however, were willing to enter missions or allow Spanish presence in their territory. Native groups such as the Comanche or Apache sometimes attacked missions, and priests eventually abandoned several missions that had no soldiers to defend them. The Spanish cattle from these closed missions became wild and multiplied so that by the mid-1700s many thousands of wild cattle lived in the Southwestern region.

In 1776, Spain centralized power in its northern frontier by combining Texas, New Mexico, Arizona, and the northern

▲ Mission San Jose de Tumacacori in Santa Cruz, Arizona, was founded by Father Eusebio Kino in the late 1600s. Father Kino converted more than 4,000 American Indians to Catholicism and taught his converts to become vaqueros.

provinces of Mexico into one area named Las Provincias Internas. Spain made Theodore de Croix the Spanish governor in charge of the region, and he was surprised by the numbers of unbranded cattle herds he found when he inspected the territory. In 1778, he began extensive government control of ranching. He claimed all unclaimed cattle for the government of Spain, and he was the first to establish strict rules in the frontier region. People had to create unique brands, buy licenses, and pay tax for any wild cow or horse they caught. They also needed permits to buy or sell meat.

▼ Vaqueros used long ropes known as reatas to catch and bring down cattle from the saddle. Southwestern cowboys later adopted these ropes—only they called their ropes lariats or lassos.

Ranching in California

Ranching arrived in present-day California in the 1760s, when Catholic Father Junípero Serra spearheaded the building of the first California missions. Cattle for the mission ranches were brought from Mexico. In 1769, on one of the first long-distance cattle drives, a crew of Mexican vaqueros traveled overland through about 600 miles (965 kilometers) of desert and mountains from Loreto, Mexico, to San Diego, California. By 1773, there were five missions in California, and each had a small herd of cattle. Between 1786 and the early 1820s, Spain made about twenty land grants to private citizens for ranching, but the missions—now twenty-one in number and managing huge cattle herds—dominated the California economy. Until the mid-1800s, ranching was the main industry in California, and cattle were so valuable that hides were nick-named "California bank-notes."

California missions initially did not let their cattle roam far. The cattle grazed near the missions during the day, and vaqueros corralled the cattle at night. Meat was plentiful, and the mission ranchos were mostly self-sustaining. Wild horses would be rounded up whenever new ones were needed, and cattle roundups happened in the spring and fall.

At first, Native Americans in the region who were forced to work in missions were not allowed to ride horses. As the cattle population increased, however, the missions had to let the cattle roam on open ranges so there would be enough grass for them to eat. There were more cattle than the vaqueros from Mexico could handle, and the priests began teaching local Native Americans how to handle cattle. Eventually, in the late 1700s, Spanish authorities stopped enforcing the law forbidding Native American horse riding. In the early 1800s, mission fathers, after being given permission by Spanish authorities, trained some talented Indian vaqueros in the arts of saddlemaking and blacksmithing (the art of making useful objects, such as horseshoes, out of metal).

▼ A statue of Junípero Serra outside the Santa Barbara Mission in California. Father Serra was a missionary for twenty years in New Spain, founding the first nine missions along the California coast.

19

Cattle rustling, or the stealing of cattle, was a problem on the New Spain frontier. Cattle rustlers often butchered the cattle, then left the meat rotting on the carcasses and sold the hides very cheaply to miners and other workers. Native American groups also raided ranches and stole cattle and horses. The Spanish tried to make peace with Native American groups by offering them gifts. They also attempted to police the frontier by building presidios, or military forts. Spain, however, did not have the funds or enough soldiers to properly staff the presidios, and most rustlers were not caught.

Ranching in Mexico

In 1810, after three hundred years of strict Spanish control, the colonists of New Spain began to fight for their freedom. After eleven years of war, on February 21, 1821, New Spain won independence from Spain and became the nation of Mexico. This event changed the region's ranching industry forever. Spain's government had tightly controlled ranching and placed many limitations on foreign trade and settlement. Mexico, unlike Spain, encouraged foreign trade and settlement. California rancheros began obtaining luxury manufactured goods, such as wine, fine cloth, and tools, from Anglo traders on ships that stopped along the coasts to trade for hides and tallow. Texas rancheros also began sending increasing numbers of cattle to French Louisiana to sell.

The era of mission ranching ended when Mexico passed the Secularization Act of 1833, which took the land and cattle away from the Catholic Church and redistributed it to citizens. Many priests had vaqueros quickly slaughter the missions' herds of cattle before the cattle could be confiscated by the government and sold the hides and tallow for money. Thousands of cattle were

◀ As the ranching industry grew, people from different cultures began to interact. An Anglo cowboy (left), a Native American (middle), and a Mexican vaquero (right) play a game in this 1908 photo.

slaughtered, and California's cattle population alone rapidly decreased from about 535,000 cattle in 1830 to about 28,220 cattle by 1842.

Ranching in what is now Arizona and New Mexico came almost to a standstill after the missions were closed, but the rancho system continued in northern Mexico, Texas, and California. Native American mission vaqueros went to work for private ranchers and were quickly entrapped by debt to wealthy ranch owners.

By 1835, Mexico had also made more than six hundred private land grants in its northern territories, many of them to Anglo settlers. Ranching in those regions was beginning to gradually change and blend Anglo, Spanish, and Mexican traditions.

Chapter 4

Early Anglo Ranching

Beginning in the 1830s, thousands of Anglo settlers, many from the growing United States, moved to the Texas region in search of inexpensive land. The large Mexican rancho style of cattle raising, however, was unfamiliar to them, and most Anglos used their land for farming and raised only a few livestock for food.

The decline of ranching in the area forced many Mexican vaqueros to find other means of work. Some vaqueros slaughtered wild cattle and traded the hides and tallow. Others began catching wild mustang horses and taming them. They then sold horses to Anglo settlers.

Growth of Anglo Ranching

Ranching gradually became more popular among settlers after immigration agents began promoting cattle raising in

◀ Vaquero brands cattle in the 1800s in this hand-colored illustration. Some vaqueros branded wild cattle to form their own ranches. Others traded hides and tallow.

the mid-1830s. Texas cattle were so plentiful and inexpensive—a cow with a calf cost about $10 at that time—that most people could begin livestock raising without a large investment. There was so much public land for grazing that David Woodman, in his 1835 *Guide to Texas Emigrants*, wrote, "It is believed that no country in the world presents so great temptations to the grazier as the prairies and cane-brakes of Texas afford."

▲ Most of the first Anglo ranching operations were small family businesses. Ranch houses in early Texas looked much like this typical western house, shown in 1888. In later years, wealthy cattlemen would build large, multiple-story ranch homes.

Wealthy Anglo settlers brought slaves with them, and the slaves did much of the farming and ranch work. In 1836, there were about five thousand African American slaves in Texas. With the growth in large Anglo cotton and cattle plantations, census records show that the number of slaves increased to about 182,500 by 1860. Anglos also hired Mexican vaqueros if they needed additional help with cattle.

Many Anglo settlers, however, were not wealthy people and could not afford slaves or vaqueros. A settler's family did the work, and most women worked alongside their husbands. In 1836, a Texas settler named Mary Austin Holley wrote, "It is not uncommon for ladies to mount their mustangs and hunt with their husbands, and with them to camp out for days . . . they will go fifty miles (80 km) to a ball with their silk dresses, made perhaps in Philadelphia or New Orleans, in their saddle-bags."

The Revolution and the Cowboys

By the mid-1830s, there were more than thirty thousand people in Texas, and Anglos outnumbered Mexicans three to one.

▲ Sam Houston in 1848. During the Texas Revolution, Sam Houston and a force of Texan soldiers defeated the Mexican commander and his men by surprising them during their afternoon nap on April 21, 1836.

Anglo Texans pressured Mexico to grant Texas statehood and to give them more control of the government. These issues caused conflicts between the Anglo Texans and Mexican leaders, resulting in the Texas Revolution (1835–1836).

During the Texas Revolution, some Texans raided Mexican ranches and drove away cattle. These Texan raiders became known as "cow-boys." Not everyone approved of the cowboys' activities, and some considered them to be cattle rustlers in disguise. One army officer wrote that cowboys "are all in the cow stealing business, and are scattered all over this frontier. They pretend . . . they steal only from the enemy; but I am convinced, to the contrary, that they steal from Texans as well."

In 1836, Texas won its independence and became the Republic of Texas. Mexican ranchers then fled from Texas territory. Their cattle became wild and were considered public property to be had for the taking. Sam Houston, the republic's first president, sent his soldiers to round up wild cattle to feed the army. Discharged soldiers also began rounding up the wild cattle and branding them to start their own ranches.

The new Republic of Texas faced many problems. The government was low on funds. Also, Mexico had never recognized Texas independence, so Texans lived under a constant threat of invasion by Mexican troops. To strengthen its political and financial position, Texas joined the United States in December 1845.

Mexico, however, had never agreed to its borders with Texas and warned the United States that annexation of Texas would be considered an act of war. After Texas became a state, Mexico sent troops into Texas and killed U.S. scouts, thus starting the Mexican-American War (1846–1848). The United States won the war in 1848 and gained possession of half of Mexico's territory, including present-day Arizona, New Mexico, and California.

Gold Rush and Northern Ranchos

An event on January 24, 1848, brought about the sudden end of the rancho era in northern California. Gold was discovered at Sutter's sawmill on the American River near Coloma, California.

In 1848, ranchos still covered about 13 million acres (5 million ha) of California, but mining

▲ Prospectors panning for gold in 1889. The Gold Rush's influx of people to California created a huge market for beef.

quickly replaced ranching as California's main industry. By 1850, more than one hundred thousand gold seekers had rushed to California. Thousands of gold seekers disregarded the rancheros' legal property rights and moved onto rancho land as squatters, digging for gold and stealing cattle to eat. Rancheros tried to save their ranchos by taking the squatters to court.

In 1851, Congress placed the burden of proving land ownership on the Spaniards and Mexicans. Anglo immigrants needed only two signatures on petitions to gain claim to supposedly "vacant" rancho land. Proving rancheros' land ownership was costly and took as long as seventeen years. By the time the cases were settled, most rancheros were already bankrupt and could no longer afford to keep their land.

▶ A cattle drive in the early 1900s takes on a typical formation as the cowboys coax the herd into following a lead steer.

California Drives of the 1850s

The population explosion during the Gold Rush opened a huge market in California for meat. Prices jumped as high as $75 per cow in San Francisco, and for the first time, cattle were more valuable for beef than for hides and tallow.

Rancheros in southwest regions quickly began the northward movement of their cattle. Vaqueros drove herds of about one thousand cattle each on trails along the California coast or through the San Joaquin Valley to sell in northern markets. They hauled their supplies in carts and slept in tents or in the open on blankets. They bought food from settlers or Native Americans if they ran out of supplies and killed cattle—called a "beef" or "beeves" by cowhands—when they needed fresh meat.

In Texas, cattle sold for just $1 to $2 each. Texas ranchers figured they could lose half of their herd on the long trip to

"Wore Out with Fatigue"

Driving cattle on a trail was dangerous and hard work, and weak cattle were left behind to die. The hours spent riding horses were physically demanding, and there were the constant threats of bad weather, raids, or stampedes. Cowboys who became sick and did not recover were buried along the trail. Cyrus C. Loveland describes his 1850 cattle drive from Missouri to the California gold fields in a diary.

May 23, 1850
Last night we lost no cattle but have nearly every other night. Found a human skeleton with a pair of shoes on it.

July 4, 1850
We killed a beef and had a fine spot of soup, which was the best of anything that we have had on the trip. We also had a desert [sic] of peach pie which really reminded me of home.

September 5, 1850
Never was this party so completely used up as when we came in from the desert. We were so wore out with fatigue and for want of sleep that like many of the old crows it might have been said of us that we were give out, for we had been without sleep two days and nearly all of two nights and on the go constantly. The last night on the desert we were so overcome with sleep that we were obliged to get off our horses and walk for fear of falling off. As we were walking along after the cattle it certainly would have been very amusing to anyone who could see us astaggering along against each other, first on one side of the road, then the other, like a company of drunken men.

California and still make a profit. In 1848, several ranchers began moving huge herds of Texas longhorns to California. Many of the cattle drivers, known as "drovers," were gold seekers desiring to travel to California. They worked the cattle drives for no wages—just in exchange for the food and protection they needed for the five- to six-month trip to reach California.

Ranchers drove so many cattle to California that the market flooded, and the overstock reduced the price of beef to about $18 by 1855. A drought in 1856 forced ranchers to sell even more cattle in poor condition. In 1857, the California cattle market collapsed. Ranchers again needed new markets for beef.

Chapter 5

Texas Fever and the Civil War

The search for markets for their ever-expanding herds was a constant challenge to U.S. ranch owners, especially those in Texas. Some Texas ranchers had tried to ship cattle in boats sailing in the Gulf of Mexico, but this proved time-consuming and expensive. The success of the California drives made other ranchers realize that it was possible to move cattle long distances, and in the 1850s, they began to travel new overland routes to the north.

The Northeast Trail

Most Texas drovers began the long journey northeast by following the Shawnee Trail, also called the Kansas or Osage Trail. The trail traveled north

◀ These cowboys are herding cattle to market on a cattle drive in the late 1800s.

from Texas and crossed what is now eastern Oklahoma, then known as Indian Territory. Native Americans from the East had been forcibly relocated to Indian Territory, and Anglos had to receive their permission to enter their land, which often involved paying a toll for each head of cattle. After Indian Territory, the drovers entered southwest Missouri and herded the cattle to St. Louis, the only cattle market west of the Allegheny Mountains. Those who chose not to sell the cattle in St. Louis continued to travel east.

As in California, Texas cattle sold for much more money in northeast markets than in Texas. Texas cattle were inexpensive because the only upkeep was the cost of herding and branding them. The grass and water the cattle needed were free. Soon, thousands of Texas cattle were making the trip northeast.

Some Native Americans, who disliked Anglos entering Indian Territory, raided the trail herds, but most Indians were peaceful and charged tolls, ranging from 10 cents to 75 cents per head of cattle that crossed their land.

Cattle Trails

CANADA

MT
ND
ID
SD
MN
WY
Cheyenne
NE
IA
UT
CO
Denver
KS
Topeka
Kansas City
Sedalia
Ellsworth
Abilene
MO
AZ
NM
Red R.
OK
AR
TX
LA
San Antonio
Gulf of Mexico
Rio Grande R.
MEXICO

LEGEND
~ River
• Settlement
🐄 Cattle Raising Country
— Cattle Trail
Forested Lands
Arid Lands
Grasslands
— Present-day State Borders

0   200 mi
0   300 km

▲ This map shows the major cattle trails throughout the Southwest in the mid-1800s.

29

Thomas Ponting

Thomas Ponting was one of the first people to transport cattle from Texas to the East Coast. In 1853, he began herding about seven hundred eighty longhorns on the Shawnee Trail across Indian Territory. He and his men traveled in a wagon pulled by a lead ox that wore a bell around its neck, and the cattle followed the sound of the bell.

In the spring of 1854, they reached central Illinois and sold most of the cattle there. They kept about one hundred fifty of the best and herded them to Muncie, Indiana, where they built a ramp and loaded them onto railroad cars that had never before been used to transport cattle. They led the cattle to grass at the railroad stops and finally sold them in New York. Cattle buyers had never seen that breed of cow and thought the Texas longhorns were from Iowa.

A New York reporter wrote an article about the arrival of the Texas cattle for the *Daily Tribune*, saying, "Another thing is demonstrated in the yards to-day, which proves that cattle can be brought two thousand miles (3,218 km) with profit to the drovers, and sold at such prices as prevail to-day. We have a drove of Texas cattle."

Texas Fever

In the early 1850s, just when it seemed Texas ranchers had finally discovered markets for their herds, they faced a new obstacle. Their cattle breed, known as Texas longhorns or Spanish cattle, were blamed for a disease called "Texas fever" or "Spanish fever," a fever of the spleen caused by a tick common to Southern areas. Until 1889, people did not know that ticks carried the disease and tried to keep Texas longhorns away from their fields and cattle.

Texas longhorns usually remained unaffected by Texas fever. The ticks, however, spread to other cattle that came in contact with the longhorns, and these other breeds caught the disease. Cattle with Texas fever staggered as they walked, arched their backs, hung their heads, and had dull, glassy eyes. Thousands of cattle in Missouri died from Texas fever. In 1855, the state's legislature passed a law stating that no Texas cattle infected with the disease or suspected of carrying the disease could enter Missouri. Kansas passed similar laws in 1859.

For a time, however, Texas cattle were still allowed to enter Missouri as long as they showed no sign of the disease, but ticks spread to the landscape, and other breeds of cattle traveling the same territory became sick. Farmers in Missouri, Kansas, and other states north of Texas formed armed groups that kept watch for Texas longhorns. By 1858, after more outbreaks, armed groups in Kansas and Missouri began turning back even the healthy-looking Texas longhorns. One Missouri newspaperman supported the farmers' actions, saying, "No one can for a moment blame the citizens of Missouri for adopting summary measures to protect their stock from the fearful ravages of Spanish fever."

Texans continued to herd their cattle to market, but they shifted their trails farther west to avoid populated areas with armed and angry farmers.

The Civil War

All the progress of cattle ranchers in Texas and throughout the United States came to a sudden standstill in 1861. That year, the Civil War (1861–1865) erupted between Northern states that wanted to outlaw slavery and supported a strong federal government and Southern states that left the Union because they favored states' rights and wanted to keep slavery legal.

Northern herds were drastically reduced as cattle were slaughtered to

▼During the Civil War, cattle herds were slaughtered to feed soldiers, such as these New York Infantry troops in 1863.

feed Union troops. People in the South, including Texans, gave their cattle to feed Confederate forces, asking only to be paid for the cost of transporting them. The flow of Texas cattle to troops stopped after Union forces blockaded key areas, such as the Mississippi River, in an attempt to stop the transport of cattle in the South.

Texas ranches suffered greatly during the Civil War because they were not self-sufficient like other homesteads that combined farming and ranching. Many women began planting gardens, and some drove small herds to Mexico to sell.

Lack of resources caused by so many men leaving to fight led to the majority of cattle roaming wild during the war. Most new calves were unbranded. Natural disasters—such as winter storms and a terrible drought that lasted from 1861 to 1863— killed thousands of cattle. Herds drifted hundreds of miles (km) from their home ranges in search of water and food.

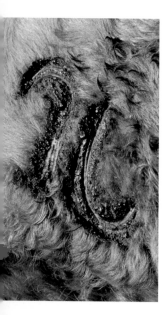

▼ This calf has a fresh brand burned onto its left flank.

Cow Hunts and Mavericks

After the war ended in 1865, most ranchers returned home to find their cattle dead or scattered. To restore their herds, ranchers banded together and conducted numerous cow hunts. They searched thousands of miles (km) to find cattle with their brand on them and drove them home.

After the war, thousands of mavericks, or unbranded cattle, roamed the Southwest, especially Texas. The term *maverick* originated in about 1845, when a Texas leader named Samuel Maverick accepted a herd of four hundred cattle for payment of a debt. He had little interest in ranching and neglected his livestock. As his herd grew, the new calves remained unbranded. People living near

Maverick soon began to refer to all unbranded cattle as "one of Maverick's." By the end of the Civil War, Texans referred to all unbranded cattle as mavericks. To supplement their herds, returning soldiers branded whatever mavericks they could find, which were considered public property.

Rustling

By 1870, most mavericks had been branded, and people began to steal cattle by sneaking onto ranges, taking unbranded calves away from their mothers, and placing their own brands on them. This illegal kind of rustling became known as "mavericking."

Some people stole cattle by changing the owners' brands to their own brands. These rustlers used a thick wire or a running iron—which was a straight rod with a curve at the end—to artfully change the owners' brands into the rustlers' own brands. Officials outlawed running irons because rustling was such a problem, and anyone caught with one was charged with rustling.

There were few or no law agencies in the open range, and cowboys often owned guns to protect cattle. Most cattle ranchers enforced their own justice and often hung rustlers with no trial.

▲ Dakota Territory cowboys rope and brand cattle in 1891. Roping and branding were hard work wherever they were done. Andy Adams, a cowboy in 1905, wrote of the cowboy life, "If I have any word to say of these range riders, it is that no harder life is lived by any working man."

Chapter 6

The Cattle Boom

Like gold fever changed life in California, "cattle fever" changed the entire Southwest. After the Civil War, there was a huge demand for beef in the East because most northern herds had been killed to feed soldiers. The expansion of the railroad and the invention of refrigerated cars made it possible to ship cattle from Kansas to slaughterhouses farther north and east where meat was packed and then shipped in refrigerated railroad cars to markets. Ranchers in the Southwest, especially Texans, had more than enough cattle to supply the Northerners' taste for beef. In fact, an 1860 census concluded that about one-eighth of the cattle in the United States, 3.5 million, lived in Texas. In the 1860s, thanks to the railroads, there was finally a way to send cattle

◀ Cowboys were the main labor force during the cattle boom. In this 1880 picture, they are rounding up cattle on the open range in Texas.

from the south to the northeast and northwest markets. The cattle boom began.

▲ On May 10, 1869, at Promontory Summit, Utah, workers celebrated the joining of the rails of the Transcontinental Railroad, which linked the West and East Coasts.

The Railroad and the Cattle Boom

In 1862, Congress agreed to partially fund a Transcontinental Railroad that would stretch the length of the country. Railroad crews laid thousands of miles of track across western regions, including Kansas. If Texas and other Southwestern ranchers could transport their cattle to railroad lines in Kansas, they had—for the first time—a cheap and easy way to ship their cattle to eastern markets.

The railroad also hastened westward settlement. Thousands of workers, consisting mainly of African Americans and Chinese and European immigrants, cleared the land and built the railroad tracks. These workers brought greater diversity to the Western population. Towns formed along railroad stops, and the trains quickly brought hundreds of new settlers out West. Most of these settlers claimed a homestead under the Homestead Act of 1862. This law stated that legal settlers could receive title to 160 acres (65 ha) of public land for free if they lived there for five years and farmed and improved their claim.

▶ More than forty thousand buffalo hides are ready to be shipped to market from Dodge City, Kansas, in 1878. Buffalo hides could be used to make coats and other clothing, as well as blankets. The thick "wool" holds warmth better than many other kinds of animal fur.

Decline of Buffalo

Cattle ranching could not have expanded at this time without the grazing ranges opened by the decline of buffalo. Estimates claim that about 60 million buffalo once roamed the United States' grass-covered Great Plains, and Native American groups depended on the animals for their survival.

As more Anglos moved onto the Great Plains in the 1860s, buffalo hunting became a widely practiced and profitable business, and hunters slaughtered millions of buffalo. People ground the bones of the buffalo into fertilizer and used the valuable hides to make clothes and industrial products, such as pulleys. Over-hunting decreased the buffalo population to drastically low levels approaching extinction.

Many Plains Indian groups noticed that the arrival of the railroad reduced wild game and buffalo in their hunting grounds. Some Native Americans tried to protect their way of life by attacking the railroad crews and Anglo settlers. The United States built new forts in western regions and sent soldiers to control Native American uprisings. The government eventually broke its treaties with Native American groups and forcibly removed them from the Plains to reservations in the Northwest. The Great Plains were then opened to Anglos for the expansion of farming and cattle ranching, and the new settlements and reservations became additional markets for beef.

Cattlemen

New ranches soon occupied former Native American land. Wealthy investors, known as cattlemen, bought thousands of acres and formed huge ranches. Cattlemen were powerful and controlled water sources on ranges and wrote rules governing their ranches.

Foreign investors in England and Scotland heard of the money to be made in Texas cattle and invested in large ranches that they operated like corporations. Two of the most famous ranch corporations were the Chicago-owned XIT and the Scottish-owned Matador. Corporate ranches hired local managers to oversee ranching operations.

◀ This cowboy (c. 1890–1920) is wearing chaps to protect his legs from dense underbrush. Although most cowboys were Anglo Americans, by the late 1800s a substantial number were African Americans or Mexican vaqueros.

A Cowboy's Tools

Many of a cowboy's tools and techniques were adapted from vaqueros. Saddles were patterned after vaquero's saddles and had large horns in front and a high cantle in back. Cowboys used long, braided rawhide ropes called lariats, which were similar to the vaqueros' reatas. Like the vaquero, the cowboy wore boots and chaps—heavy leather trousers without a seat—over his pants to protect his legs from rough brush. The cowboy used small metal spurs attached to his boot to urge his horse forward, while the vaquero used larger metal spurs. Cowboys wore wide-brimmed hats, similar to the vaquero's sombrero, to shield their eyes from the Sun and bandannas around their necks to wipe sweat or shield their faces from dust.

Cowboys used roping techniques learned from vaqueros. A cowboy would use his lariat to make a lasso, or loop of rope, which he threw over a cow's horns or around its legs. He then stopped his horse, and the loop tightened around the cow, which made it fall to the ground. They also practiced the open-range grazing, branding, earmarking, and roundups that the Spanish pioneered.

The Cowboy

During the cattle boom era, the term cowboy first began to be used to describe skilled cowhands. Cowboys worked up to fourteen hours each day. There were about thirty-five thousand cowboys working on the range and an estimated one-third of them were Mexican vaqueros or African American cowboys. A few Native American cowboys worked on ranches in Indian Territory.

Instead of working for just one ranch owner, cowboys often hired onto any crew that was hiring. Cowboy work was often seasonal. In spring, they signed onto a ranch to help with the roundup. Next, they were hired by a drover and spent the summer working on a cattle drive. They returned to the ranches in time for the autumn roundup. Winter ranch work was scarce, and often cowboys lived on their summer wages or did other work in town.

The Roundup

Cattle wandered and grazed on free public grass, resulting in

herds from several ranches mingling on one range. To brand and castrate new calves, return strays to their owners, and separate the stock to be sold, ranchers held two organized roundups in spring and autumn each year. Roundups could cover up to 100 square miles (259 square kilometers) and took up to several months.

▲ During roundups and cattle drives, cowboys organized camps—like this one pictured in 1873—that often included tents and one or more supply wagons.

Cowboys from several large ranches would work together for the event, and a large roundup could have hundreds of cowboys and many wagons camped in one place. During the day, cowboys rode long hours to search the selected range for cattle and then herded them to a central location. After all the cattle in the range were gathered into one huge herd, they cut the herd, which meant separating the cattle into smaller herds by owner.

Once the herds were cut, cowboys did the hot and bloody job of branding. One cowboy rode horseback and used a lasso to rope and down a calf. A second cowboy on foot dragged the fallen calf to the branding fire and held it still while a third cowboy took a red-hot branding iron and burned its mother's brand onto its flank. The calf was dehorned and earmarked, then released back into the herd. Selected male calves were also castrated, while others were kept intact for breeding purposes.

At night, cowboys sang songs, told stories, and engaged in friendly roping and riding competitions. The modern rodeo descended from these nighttime roundup activities.

Chapter 7

Cattle Drives

As ranges in the Southwest began to overcrowd with cattle in the 1870s, ranchers bought land in the Plains and Northwest and moved herds there to feed. They shipped beef wherever there was a market, including mining boom-towns in Nevada and Colorado.

The location of cattle trails depended on the quarantine line, which was created to protect northern cattle from Texas fever and farmers' fields from being trampled by cattle. The location of the quarantine line moved westward several times as increasing amount of settlers claimed homesteads and began farming. Depending on their final destination, cattle drovers used two main trails to towns in Kansas—the Chisolm Trail to Abilene or the Western Trail to Dodge City.

Cattle Drives

Some ranch owners organized cattle drives themselves, while others hired specialized contractors who were paid

◀ Cowboys were famous for singing to calm cattle, and some cowboys formed bands. The Dodge City Cow-Boy Band, shown here in 1885, toured the United States.

up to $1.50 for each head of cattle they transported from Texas to Kansas. Contractors could make a large profit on a herd—if nothing went wrong. Before being driven to market, a trail herd was led through a chute and given a special trail brand in addition to the ranch owner's brand to help cowboys sort cattle that became mixed with other herds.

A trail crew consisted of a trail boss who was in charge of establishing the route, finding grazing areas and watering spots, paying tolls, establishing camp rules, buying supplies, and paying salaries. The trail boss hired a team of at least ten or more cowboys, depending on the number of cattle to be moved. Each crew had a remuda, which was a herd of thirty or more horses. Several times during the day, cowboys placed their tired horses in the remuda and selected fresh remounts to ride. A wrangler (person who tends horses), usually a teenager with little trail experience, made sure the horses were fed and herded them along the trail during the day and placed them in rope corrals at night.

Fat cattle were much more valuable than thin cattle, so trail bosses moved the herds slowly to keep them from losing weight. Most herds followed a lead steer while traveling up to 15 miles (24 km) per day. A pair of experienced cowboys rode one on each side of the lead steer to guide the way and keep pace. Other cowboys rode back and forth along the middle of the herd. The least experienced cowboys were stuck with the dusty and dirty job of riding behind the herd to push the slow cattle forward. At night, cowboys gathered the cattle in one place and took turns working guard-duty shifts. They often sang to help keep the cattle calm. They also rode circles around the herd to keep it from straying.

An older man, sometimes a retired cowboy, was the cook. His job was to cook meals, ride ahead of the herd to set up camp, and drive the mules that pulled the chuck wagon, which was a heavy-

▲ These cowboys are gathered around the chuck wagons in 1905 to eat breakfast before beginning their day herding cattle.

duty wagon invented expressly for roundups and cattle drives. Its main feature was the chuck box, which had compartments for food supplies and a hinged lid that folded down to make a work table for the cook. A water barrel strapped to the side of the wagon provided drinking water. Camp meals consisted of nonperishable foods, such as coffee, beans, sugar, and bacon.

Cowboys faced many dangers while out on the trail. There was the constant threat of stampedes by frightened cattle. During a stampede, most often caused by thunder, cattle would run forward madly and trample anything in their path. A herd might be so scattered by stampedes that cowboys could spend weeks looking for them. Some trails had several dangerous river crossings, and many cowboys drowned when their horses stumbled while trying to urge cattle to swim across swollen rivers. Some rivers were known for special hazards, such as the quicksand of the South Canadian.

Cow Towns

Cowboys were paid in cash at the end of the trail, receiving about $30 for one month's work. Most cowboys quickly spent their wages on baths, new clothes, fine food, drink, and other entertainment in the cow towns where the railheads were.

Cow towns quickly formed, and sometimes quickly died, depending on the ever-shifting quarantine line and the railroad's expansion. All cow towns were home to a railroad depot, stockyards, stables, hotels, stores, and numerous saloons where cowboys could drink, dance, and gamble.

End of the Cattle Boom

The invention of barbed wire in 1873 brought the open-range system of ranching to an end by 1889. During the fence-cutter wars, supporters of free grazing roamed the ranges at night and cut miles (km) of fences. This resulted in a sometimes bloody fight between powerful ranchers and fence-cutters. Finally, officials passed laws that made it illegal to cut fences—thus ending the era of free grass, common grazing ranges, roundups, and cattle drives.

Meanwhile, the cattle boom was coming to an end. By the late 1880s, greedy ranchers had overstocked the ranges, and millions of cattle could not find enough to eat. Hundreds of thousands of cattle died during the harsh winter of 1886, and ranchers tried to recoup their losses by sending large herds in poor condition to market in 1887. The surplus cattle made beef prices fall dramatically. Most ranchers went bankrupt. The surviving ranchers reorganized the industry—reducing herds so the ranges could recover, fencing pastures, and feeding their cattle during winter.

▼ These cowboys are celebrating their arrival in the cow town of Newton, Kansas, in 1908.

The cattle boom lasted for just about twenty years but forever changed the American West. By 1885, a government report claimed that about 44 percent of U.S. land was used for ranching. The boom had transformed the landscape by encouraging the westward movement of settlers who built new cow towns, trails, and railroad lines to handle the growing cattle industry.

The expansion of the railroad, which aided the cattle boom, and the shipping of food from one part of the country to another helped achieve Manifest Destiny. In the process, different regions of the country were linked and became interdependent on each other for goods.

The growth of the cattle industry and the westward movement, however, came at a great cost. Cattle replaced buffalo on the Plains, and Native American territory was seized by the government and sold to ranchers or given to homesteaders.

In Western movies, books, and songs, the open range now represents limitless possibility and the American dream. The myth of the cowboy evolved into a popular hero who represents the American ideal of personal freedom. In reality, the cowboy was low on the social order, and his life was full of hard work and little pay.

Dark Days

Cowboy George Duffield wrote ab his experiences driving cattle from Texas to Iowa in 1866.

" May 1st: Travelled 10 mile. Corryell co. Big stampede. Lost head of cattle.

May 2nd: Spent the day hunting found but 25 head. It has been r ing for three days. These are da days for me.

May 13th: Big thunder storm las night. Stampede. Lost 100 beev Hunted all day. Found 50. All tire Everything discouraging.

May 20th: Rain poured down for hours. Ground in a flood. Creeks up—Hands leaving. Gloomy tim ever I saw. Drove 8 miles with 5 hands (359 head).

May 31st: Swimming cattle is th order. We worked all day in the r & at dusk got the last beefe ove am now out of Texas—This day long be remembered by me—Th was one of our party drowned to (Mr. Carr) & several narrow esca & I among the no.

June 23rd. Worked all day hard the river trying to make the bee swim & did not get one over. Ha go back to prairie sick & discou aged. Have not got the Blues bu in Hel of a fix. "

1492: ▶ Columbus lands in the Americas and claims the land for Spain.

1493: ▶ First cattle and horses arrive in Western Hemisphere.

1521: ▶ First cattle and horses arrive in Americas.

1529: ▶ The Spanish establish the Mesta, the first stockowner's association in Americas.

1574: ▶ Mesta rules that no Native American, mulatto, mestizo, or slave can own a horse.

1598: ▶ Ranching reaches the territory that would become New Mexico.

1687: ▶ Ranching reaches the territory that would become Arizona.

1690: ▶ Ranching reaches the territory that would become Texas.

1769: ▶ Ranching reaches the territory that would become California.

1803: ▶ The Louisiana Purchase doubles the size of the United States.

1810: ▶ Mexican Revolution begins after Miguel Hidalgo calls for rebellion from Spain.

1821: ▶ Mexico wins independence from Spain, and the Mexican Revolution ends.

1834: ▶ Mexico passes law demanding that missions be secularized.

1835: ▶ Texas Revolution begins with the Battle of Gonzales.

1836: ▶ Texas Revolution ends.

1845: ▶ John O'Sullivan first uses term Manifest Destiny; Texas becomes a state.

1846: ▶ Mexican-American War begins.

1848: ▶ January 24—James Marshall finds gold at Sutter's Mill.
February 2—Mexican-American War ends when Treaty of Guadalupe Hidalgo is signed.

1850: ▶ California becomes a state.

1855: ▶ Missouri passes laws prohibiting Texas longhorns suspected of carrying Texas fever from entering the state.

1859: ▶ Kansas passes laws prohibiting Texas longhorns suspected of carrying Texas fever from entering the state.

1861: ▶ Civil War begins.

1862: ▶ The Homestead Act becomes law.

1864: ▶ Nevada becomes a state.

1865: ▶ Civil War ends.

1867: ▶ United States buys present-day Alaska from Russia.

1869: ▶ The Transcontinental Railroad is completed.

1873: ▶ Barbed wire is invented.

1889: ▶ Scientists discover that ticks carry Texas fever.

1900: ▶ Hawaii becomes a U.S. territory.

1907: ▶ Oklahoma becomes a state.

1912: ▶ New Mexico and Arizona become states.

Anglo: person of non-Spanish, European descent

annexation: to add territory into an existing political unit, such as a country, state, county, or city

brand: a mark indicating identity or ownership, burned on the hide of an animal with a hot iron

chaps: heavy leather trousers without a seat, worn over ordinary trousers by cowboys to protect their legs

colony: area, settlement, or country owned or controlled by another nation

economy: system of producing and distributing goods and services

hacienda: a huge business estate formed by a Spanish government land grant that was usually used for mining, ranching, lumbering, or farming

livestock: domestic animals, such as cattle or horses, raised for home use or for profit

manifest: obviously true and easily recognizable. The term Manifest Destiny meant that the true and obvious destiny of the United States was to expand its borders to the Pacific Ocean.

mission: center built to establish Spanish settlement, convert Native Americans to Catholicism, and exploit their slave labor

presidio: military fort built by the Spanish

Pueblo: any of some twenty-five Native American peoples living in established villages in northern and western New Mexico and northeast Arizona

rancho: Spanish word for ranch

range: an extensive area of open land on which livestock wander and graze

remount: a fresh horse used as a replacement for a tired horse

remuda: a herd of remount horses

republic: nation that has no sovereign or other unelected ruler but is led by a leader, or group of officials led by its citizens

round up (roundup): the act of herding together of cattle for inspection, branding, or shipping; event where cattle are gathered

running iron: a straight rod with a curve at the end used to draw brands on animals

rustler: a person who steals livestock, especially cattle

secularize: make nonreligious

spur: a short spike or spiked wheel that attaches to the heel of a rider's boot and is used to urge a horse forward

stampede: a sudden frenzied rush of panic-stricken animals

vaquero: a cowhand

Books

Cefrey, Holly. *From Slave to Cowboy : the Nat Love Story.* Great Moments in American History (series). New York: Rosen Central Primary Source, 2004.

Freedman, Russell. *In the Days of the Vaqueros: America's First True Cowboys.* New York: Clarion Books, 2001.

George, Charles, and Linda George. *Texas.* Seeds of a Nation (series). San Diego.: Kidhaven Press, 2002.

Isaacs, Sally Senzel. *Cattle Trails and Cowboys.* The American Adventure (series). Chicago: Heinemann Library, 2004.

King, David. *American Voices: Westward Expansion.* American Heritage, American Voices (series). Hoboken, N.J.: John Wiley & Sons, 2003.

Randolph, Ryan P. *Black Cowboys.* The Library of the Westward Expansion (series). New York: PowerKids Press, 2003.

Web Sites

America's West
http://www.americanwest.com/index2.htm

Cattle Raisers Museum
http://www.texascattleraisers.org/foundation.asp

Devil's Rope Barbed Wire Museum
http://www.barbwiremuseum.com/

The Handbook of Texas Online
www.tsha.utexas.edu/handbook/online/articles/view/HH/fho73.html

Kansas Cattle Towns
http://www.kansascattletowns.com/index.html

National Cowboy and Western Heritage Museum
http://www.cowboyhalloffame.org/

PBS—The West
http://www.pbs.org/weta/thewest/program/

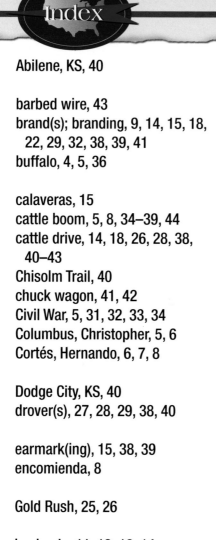